Disgusting Foods

BY CONNIE COLWELL MILLER

Capstone press®

Mankato, Minnesota

Blazers is published by Capstone Press,
151 Good Counsel Drive, P.O. Box 669, Mankato, Minnesota 56002.
www.capstonepress.com

Library of Congress Cataloging-in-Publication Data
Miller, Connie Colwell, 1976–
    Disgusting foods / by Connie Colwell Miller.
    p. cm.—(Blazers. That's disgusting!)
    Includes bibliographical references and index.
    ISBN-13: 978-0-7368-6799-3 (hardcover)
    ISBN-10: 0-7368-6799-6 (hardcover)
    ISBN-13: 978-0-7368-7877-7 (softcover pbk.)
    ISBN-10: 0-7368-7877-7 (softcover pbk.)
    1. Food—Miscellanea—Juvenile literature. I. Title. II. Series.
TX355.M446 2007
641.3—dc22   2006026402

Summary: Describes 10 disgusting foods people eat and what makes them gross.

Editorial Credits
Mandy Robbins, editor; Thomas Emery, designer; Bob Lentz, illustrator;
    Jo Miller, photo researcher/photo editor

Photo Credits
AP/Wide World Photos/Leslie Mazoch, 16–17
Art Directors/Helene Rogers, 8, 21 (inset)
Aurora/ David McLain, 26–27, 27 (inset); IPN/Michael Freeman, 15
Corbis/ Colin McPherson, 20–21; epa/Heng Sinith, 19 (inset); Owen Franken, 6–7,
    18–19; PhotoCuisine, 11 (inset); Sygma/ Eric Preau, 10–11; Patrick Robert, cover
Grant Heilman Photography/ Photo Network Stock, 13
Index Stock Imagery/Greg Smith, 5; Henryk T. Kaiser, 28–29
Shutterstock/ Amee Cross, 7 (inset); Quayside, 9 (inset); WizData, inc., 25
SuperStock/ age fotostock, 22–23

1 2 3 4 5 6 12 11 10 09 08 07

Table of Contents

That's Disgusting!

No two people like the same foods. One person's favorite dish is another's upset stomach.

GROSS-O-METER

Use this meter to gauge how disgusting these foods really are.

THAT'S DISGUSTING

To us, cats are pets. But in some parts of the world cats are eaten like pigs or cattle.

Leg Up!

In many countries people dine on frog legs. They fry or grill the legs and eat the meat off the bone.

GROSS-O-METER

SORT OF DISGUSTING

No Fast Food

GROSS-O-METER

SORT OF DISGUSTING

Escargot is boiled snails. These chewy treats are scooped from their shells and flavored with butter.

Egg Jam

Caviar is clumps of fish eggs. People around the world spread caviar on bread, toast, or crackers.

GROSS-O-METER

SORT OF DISGUSTING

Caviar is a fancy dish.
It can cost more than
$1,000 for a small can.

Hot Dog!

Did you know that hot dogs are made of ground-up animal parts? Some hot dogs may contain bits of pig snouts and ears.

GROSS-O-METER

SORT OF DISGUSTING

Hopping Good Snacks

In South America, grasshoppers and crickets are roasted and eaten like peanuts. People say they taste like green peppers.

GROSS-O-METER

PRETTY DISGUSTING

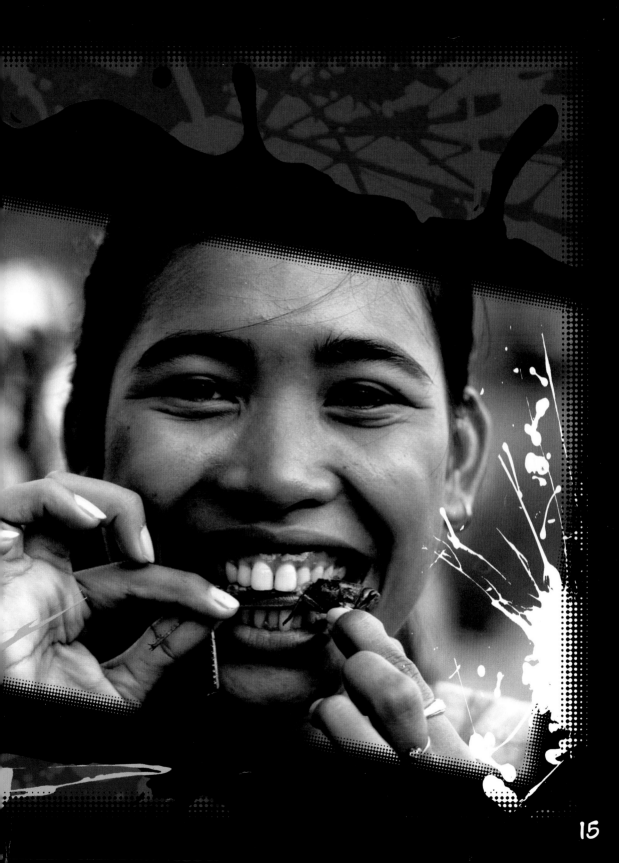

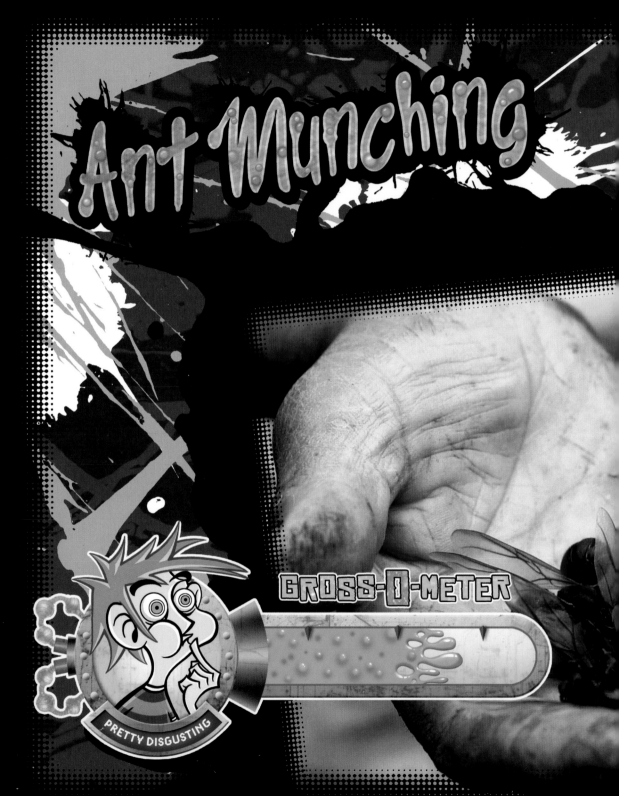

Ant Munching

GROSS-O-METER

PRETTY DISGUSTING

In Colombia, South America, moviegoers skip the popcorn. They eat bags of toasted ants instead!

BLAZER FACT

Many people say ants taste like beef jerky.

Eight-Legged Entrée

GROSS-O-METER

PRETTY DISGUSTING

In Cambodia, people munch on tarantulas. The hairy critters are fried with garlic salt and gobbled up.

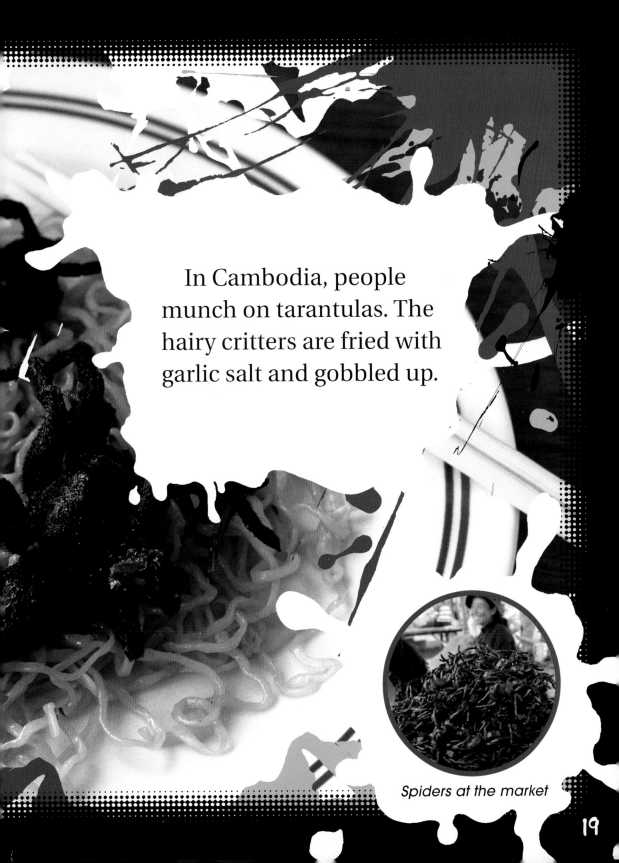

Spiders at the market

That Takes Guts!

Haggis is Scotland's national dish. Bits of sheep heart and lungs are stuffed into sheep guts with oatmeal and seasoning and boiled.

GROSS-O-METER

REALLY DISGUSTING

Ready to eat!

Pig Pudding

GROSS-O-METER

REALLY DISGUSTING

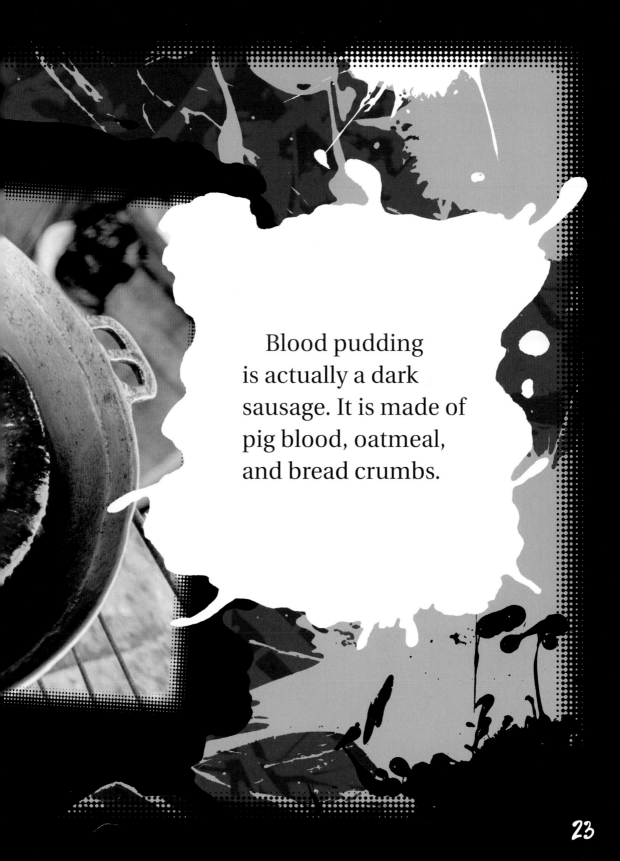

Blood pudding
is actually a dark
sausage. It is made of
pig blood, oatmeal,
and bread crumbs.

Wiggle While You Eat

Koreans dine on octopus tentacles. A chef slices them off a live octopus. The tentacles keep wiggling as a person eats them!

GROSS-O-METER

REALLY DISGUSTING

BLAZER FACT

People can feel the tentacles' suction cups pulling as they swallow.

Cheese, Please!

GROSS-O-METER

REALLY DISGUSTING

On the Mediterranean island of Sardinia, people let flies lay eggs on cheese. After the eggs hatch, people spread the maggots and cheese on bread and eat it.

Maggot cheese

Bacteria for Breakfast

Around the world, lots of people think yogurt is gross. After all, yogurt is bacteria served cold.

People might eat foods that you think are gross. But some of the things you eat are more disgusting than you think.

We made it through, and I have one thing to say. That's disgusting!

Glossary

bacteria (bak-TIHR-ee-uh)—very small living things that exist all around you and inside you; some bacteria cause disease.

caviar (KAV-ee-ahr)—the salted eggs of a large fish, usually served as an appetizer

escargot (ess-car-GO)—a snail prepared for use as food

maggot (MAG-uht)—worm-like form of a fly after it hatches from an egg; maggots are also called larvae.

tentacle (TEN-tuh-kuhl)—a long, flexible arm of an animal

Read More

Martineau, Susan. *Gruesome Grub and Disgusting Dishes.* Los Angeles: Lowell House, 2000.

Masoff, Joy. *Oh, Yuck! The Encyclopedia of Everything Nasty.* New York: Workman, 2000.

Szpirglas, Jeff. *Gross Universe: Your Guide to All Disgusting Things Under the Sun.* Toronto: Maple Tree Press, 2004.

Internet Sites

FactHound offers a safe, fun way to find Internet sites related to this book. All of the sites on FactHound have been researched by our staff.

Here's how:

1. Visit *www.facthound.com*

2. Choose your grade level.

3. Type in this book ID **0736867996** for age-appropriate sites. You may also browse subjects by clicking on letters, or by clicking on pictures and words.

4. Click on the **Fetch It** button.

FactHound will fetch the best sites for you!

Index